From Chicago to Spinoza

Also by Robert Tosei Osterman

A Clear Mind: One Man's Experience of Life After Lymphoma

From Chicago to Spinoza

Poems and a Play in Three Acts

ROBERT TOSEI OSTERMAN

iUniverse, Inc.
Bloomington

From Chicago to Spinoza
Poems and a Play in Three Acts

The views expressed in this work are solely those of the author and do not necessarily reflect the views of the publisher, and the publisher hereby disclaims any responsibility for them.

iUniverse books may be ordered through booksellers or by contacting:

iUniverse
1663 Liberty Drive
Bloomington, IN 47403
www.iuniverse.com
1-800-Authors (1-800-288-4677)

Because of the dynamic nature of the Internet, any web addresses or links contained in this book may have changed since publication and may no longer be valid.

Any people depicted in stock imagery provided by Thinkstock are models, and such images are being used for illustrative purposes only.

Certain stock imagery © Thinkstock.

ISBN: 978-1-4502-8230-7 (sc)
ISBN: 978-1-4502-8232-1 (dj)
ISBN: 978-1-4502-8231-4 (ebk)

Printed in the United States of America

iUniverse rev. date: 02/03/2011

To my daughters: Jeanne, Laurie, and Nicole

Where there is the present, there is the past

Contents

Preface

From Chicago to Spinoza is the offspring of an earlier proposed book whose title was *Emily and Me,* which described my journey to divorce in the summer of 2000. Emily Dickinson was the muse who inspired this earlier work; and parts of it are included in this collection of poems and a mirthful entertainment in three acts.

When an editor suggested that *Emily and Me* be culled for the good images within it, I took out the numerous fragments and non-comprehensible text; and as a result there remained an insufficient number of poems for a complete book. I had been writing poetry since 1980, so I took all of my work and chose from it those poems that seemed to me to be worth putting into a book of poetry. Yet, how does the writer choose the good ones, especially when he is so close to them?

All that I can honestly say is that herein are described the vicissitudes of an ordinary life with the common poetic themes of birth and death, of love and lost love, and of melancholy and joy.

During this journey I have tried to stop and see the sky, "Smell the roses," and look into the eyes of another.

I wish to acknowledge Robert Young, my friend and mentor, who has been a source of inspiration for me during my retirement years. Many bows to Susan Cushing, CA whose acupuncture treatments have added many pain-free years to my life.

Tosei

2010

Chicago

I WAIT

The time is vespers
In a horn-curved hall.
I draw silent symbols:
Exit signs, a dry drinking fountain,
Clean ashtray, distant clock.
I silently wait and teethe rhyme
As Rilke, as Milton teased inspirations
Into sonnets, *Paradise*, and elegies.
I silently wait for solitude and silence
To burst into spontaneous birth.

THE ENTREPRENEUR

Jimmy was seven in the second year
Of the big war; he worked
At the railroad station
In the middle of Chicago,
Sixteenth and Wood St. His job:
Take the money from the soldiers,
All dressed alike
In tan uniforms, and many of them;
And run
Down the cast-iron steps
From the tracks,
Across the marble floor
Of the large lobby,
With its high-arched ceiling.
Out the main entrance
He ran
Down the concrete sidewalk across
The street from the scrap yard
With its round
Big magnetic magnet attached to a crane
By a dirty steel cable dropping metal
Parts into a dented railroad car;
A quixotic project of birth and waste and rebirth.
He ran to the end of the block and then
Ben's Tavern, dark, with dark windows,
With round red seats, where he bought Quarts
Of beer in brown bottles in brown
Paper bags. Out the front door
Ran Jimmy across the street,
This separated
The tavern from the station, and tripped
Over the concrete curb,
With his hands outstretched
To break his fall; bags and bottles flew

3

Ahead to crash on the pavement: beer,
Glass and paper covered the walk.
He lifted himself up,
Knees and palms in pain,
And ran fast to the wooden two-story
Structure, his home, next to the chain-Link fence of the scrap
factory. In tears
He told his Dad, with waving gestures,
Of his accident; they went to the tracks
To explain and return the money;
But the soldiers, in their uniforms,
All looked alike, and the coaches
And the trains were alike also;
And Jimmy couldn't tell one face from
Another with their tented hats and
Crew-cut profiles: men on their way to war.

A MOTHER'S LOVE

My Mom taught me to make a cake
And lick the bowl real clear
Of all the chocolate
That a little boy holds dear

Mom showed me how to ride the El
All the way to the loop
We'd have our lunch at Walgreens' counter
Egg salad on toast, split pea soup

Mom took me to Marshall Fields
To see the holiday pageant
The wind-up toys and dancing angels
And to buy me a Christmas present

Mom taught me to save my nickels
In Ball canning jars
To have a bike required patience
For a few years

Mom bought me some life insurance
A quarter at a time
The man would collect his monthly premium
No matter what the clime

Mom at night would tend my fever
Let me stay home from school
She knew when I was really sick
Or just playing the fool

Mom took me to see the dentist
To have a cracked tooth pulled
It broke apart while playing football
We always laughed that it was killed

Mom told me to go to the bakery
And buy a dozen D's
And the baker—bless her heart
Gave me thirteen—just to please

Mom took me to the Brookfield Zoo
On streetcars with coal-fed stoves
There we'd eat our cotton candy
Enjoying each other's loves

THE RAG MAN

The lot glistened with bloody beets, jam,
And shattered Ball jars on brown bricks,
Coated with mortar, like cake squares.
A rat supped. Disturbed,
He ran for cover; but a rock pinned his tail,
And stripped it before my eyes;
The veiny spoon slid across the valley
And vanished in a racked barn.

The Rag Man's horse and open wagon
Shared this wooden shelter.
He lived in the upper flat of the grey house
Separated from them by a gravestone colored yard.
The horse was common brown, depressed.
The wagon, warped, sported splinters like weft;
But the axels were well greased.
A new spoke joined rim to hub, rigid,
Like a new kid on the block.
I never saw the rag man up close, only in silhouettes:
Grey-black hair trimmings
Captured in mud under a mirror
Wire hung on the east wall of the house;
Circles on shoe soles pressed
Into alley dust;
Tied bundles of clothing lying
In the loft, the wagon, the dank corners;
Tarpaper lampshades, sonorous incantations;
Pinhole-peephole pricked black windows;
Aberrations revolving above tar roofs, flat;
Grey house tones, black spaces—
A kaleidoscope of negatives,
The moon a loose light bulb.
Often as I lay peering under the rail
Of my back porch, the rag man came

Hovering above the gleaming lot—
In the blacks of Hopalong Cassidy,
The faithful companion's mask,
And the grey suit of President Roosevelt.
He was Clark Gable and Randolph Scott,
The Pullman porter and Zorro,
James Cagney, Tom Mix, the East Side Kids,
Audie Murphy, and sailors in denim
Fighting billowing carrier fires.

THE SCRAPYARD

Do you recall those electro mags
That hovered in mid-air, holding metal scraps;
And how they dumped their mess
Into short-sided railroad cars?
It was not the sound,
Or the dust, or the smell that made one pay heed,
But the empty thought that choked
The brain; it knew, it saw the future
In the air. It stood mesmerized before
The monster: unable to scream or weep.
It could not leave this mangled heap.

MEMORIES

Here they come: storm clouds
Innocent in white
High in their saddles
A scattered line, trespassing the blue
Cautiously advancing as the dew

When he was a young boy
He hid in basements and in boxes
On cellar stairs, under front porches
To spy on summer flashes
Eavesdrop, counting thunder

He was tended between books
Radio adventures
Superman and the Shadow Knows episodes
Mailed for tin whistles, secret coded code rings
Badges and glow-in-the-dark globes

REALIZATION

Grandfather fell behind a door
He was alone; he huddled on the floor
(We'd been gone a-playing)
Stoic German hearts were sore

I didn't weep a tear back then
Was not even close to ten
But my heart was shocked to see
His death did not pretend

Grandmother lost her left leg
To diabetes
She rode the city bus everyday
Just to ride the city bus

Faces in the past

MICHAEL: A BUS DRIVER

I know you poet, part of me, but black;
You lean against the brick-hard wall and slap
A hand in high-five form without a cap
Upon your curls while someone's yelling "Mac."
I know you scribe, your top, inside, and back;
You press a laugh, but deep within your map
Directs you to a higher, wider gap
From "black girls are so pretty's" hard attack.
I know you wise man, prophet, scholar, Saul.
You're hidden deep within your den; you wail;
You Grendal, slyly roaming Hrothgar's hall.
Your soup of armor, bones, and hazy pall
Coagulates inside your precious Grail,
Then saint and sinner merge in highest mall.

LUCY: TERMINAL OFFICE MANAGER

I wonder where you wander when you leave
The welcome room? I wonder if you wish
Or whistle tunes or worry on a dish
At supper as you view the willow eve?
I wonder if you wear your croon and weave
Your tales while fooling on the beach near fish
And sand and fawning under sunset bliss,
Or do you homeward run as arm to sleeve?
It's funny but I see you every day
And know not where you look or how you go
Or what you dream and why your soul's so gay.
I'm not real nosey, but you see, I play
At thoughts and wander in the haying glo—
And wonder where you wander on your way.

JACK: DISPATCHER

"Control calling three-o-one"!
There's a presence in the voice:
SIT UP, LOOK OUT it seems to shout.
One really has no choice.

My gut begins to crawl about
Like stretching on a rack;
I grasp the mike with a shaking hand
Knowing that it's Jack

I see that Jack wears many masks:
To laugh, to sing, to cry;
But when he gets upon the horn,
I think I'm going to die.

The lightening bolts and thunder too
Come crashing to the sod;
I tremble, shake, and weep a few;
I fear that Jack is God.

AL: A BUS DRIVER

Each day he boards his golden bus askew
With glasses tilted, eyes like rubber balls.
His gut protrudes and rolls like pitching yawls,
With flaying arms and ears a tint of blue.
Each day he guides his crooked, screaming crew
In fun and games and loud hypnotic calls
Which shatter storefront windows in the malls
Along the frightened road to Pleasant View.
It is a scene the way they carry on;
They have such fun; it's really hard to tell
Who's up, who's out, who's down, or who is who?
He drives them like an epileptic con,
And wheezes when his children clang his bell
All mashed around in one gigantic stew.

THE ROOM

The room is drawn to legal size:
Eight plus by fourteen long;
The walls are beige to match the trim,
And cast iron pipes for song.
The rug is green, the ceiling is white;
There is a dresser, a chair,
A desk, two tables, and not much more.
There is no bed laid bare.
Instead, the rug defines the bed:
A pad for the body, head,
A striped blanket and a red
Sleeping bag bedspread.
Beside the chair a can of paint,
Promised for the desk, remains
Unopened, like blackened wine,
Embossed with bitter stains,
Trimmed in red,
Inherited from a father fourteen
Years dead.
Of course, there are other scenes:
Portable TV,
A clock radio,
Papers, books, a brassy key,
Two calendars nailed to the block—hopes lost.
An unfinished picture gaily leans
On the molding above the window,
Painted by a daughter and her Dad:
A dream-like flow, a daylong fad.
Other sights, sighs, and groans
Are here in the closet: bicycle,
Camping gear, jar of honey,
Typewriter, boots, but no money.
After the reading
On the oval staircase of the courthouse,

His ex-wife explains,
"Knew him for nineteen years;
I never figured out who he was,
Or who he wanted to be;
Neither did he."

SHARON: ICU NURSE

Pulsating rays ascend with smoky ash,
Soot; red hot air that clogs the throat,
Tears the eyes, blisters the nose. Fingertips float:
Pink cooked mutton, brailing the steaming gash.
The smoldering beam shimmers across the slash
Wide. Scorched hair curls above the moat
Aglow with dancing forms. An eerie note
Trembles in space portending a swooning crash.
Then the sightless dash, headlong over the fire,
Straight and swift into chaos, black as black,
Unknown, unflown, echoing sterile W's.
The astonishing dawn exposes a flagellant pyre.
Come, look, and see the sputtering, lifeless flack
Evaporating now, replaced by kangaroos.

MY CHERIE

There I sat at the counter
With my gyro and my poem
Marking lines on all the words
That had no rhythm and did roam.

Where somewhere out behind my ear
I heard a voice so fully clear.
It said, "Hello, and how are you?
Are you the menu, dear?"

I laughed and turned my head away,
Embarrassed by her charm;
I hid in the pages of a book
With suspicion and alarm.

"You know we're on a date," she said,
With exuberance and life;
And when I asked her for her name,
She gave me, "Nancy," my ex-wife.

"Oh me, oh my, I'm sorry;
I hope you're not upset.
I know it's hard when you're divorced,
To leave the past, forget."

"Oh, that's OK," was my reply,
"Perhaps it's meant to be;
If we should ever fall in love,
I'll surely call you my Cherie."

The emotional past

A HERMIT MONK

Attractions to me are
Far away and forbidden
Recluse in the world
To all I simply bow

Poetry is a solitary station
In twilight
Turning cards
Surprising faces

SMALL AND HIDDEN

'Tis best to be small hidden
As a flea
To nap in jungle lushness
Contra to history

'Tis good to be the vanished
As fish beneath the sea
To be one of the rushes
Beyond Geography

'Tis wonder to leap beyond the rim
Of space and flee
To traipse beyond the stars
Of Astronomy

LOVE JUST IS

Why love?
Why do the grasses bow their heads
When the wind blows?
Why do the flowers open their faces
When the sun glows?
Why does the moon hold
On the apron of the stream?
And why does the Firmament
Double rainbow?

WOULD I SEE YOUR FACE

If I could trance away somewhere
Across a staring sea
Would my floating heart despair
Less for me?

If I could peak in a new hemisphere
Of sudden mystery
Would my silver tainted tears
Stop for me?

If I could be eye to eye with God
In Heaven's climbing tree
Would the rope of missing you
Release me?

If I could die a silent monk's death
At night, about three
Would I see your shining face
If I could see?

DO I

Do I live my life beyond my sphere
Ballooning there, bulging here?

Are there tensions in my bands
Nervous, greedy, clutching hands?

Do I within my mind debate
Mumbling all the people that I hate?

Am I relentlessly entangled
In the veil forever spangled?

FALL IS COMING

These are the days of indecision
For trees to cry or laugh
The sun and frost circle for dominion
Each wins by half and half

Fall is coming fast
The leaves in the trees can't last
The Chill is in his place
The wind picks up the pace
The corn in the field is brown
The geese are honking down
School busses visit pumpkin patches
Frosty is unlatching winter's latches.

We make tooth missing faces
Triangular eyes and nose
Cut open its head in the shape of a circle
And prudently kill it with many blows

BREAD AND CIRCUSES

Someone said there were more than
Five thousand of us
So you can imagine the long lines
By the time our turn came up
The bread was dry, the fish
Questionable, at best
And not even a cup of water
Sat around a bit, listened to this guy
Emmanuel philosophize
Suddenly, up he stands and strides off
To climb some mountain
Like—hello—surprise!
Afterwards dropped in at Levi's Place
For a few pulls of wine
Got home pretty late; wife upset, crying

THE TAVERN KEEPER

Yeah, whole bunch of 'em out there
Lounging around in that forest
Show up every year about this time
Call it the Rainy Season
I don't know, sit around, play cards
Drink some wine, I suppose
Come in here wanting me to feed 'em. Well, I don't
Traipse around town with their hands out
Their leader? Guy they call Boohi, or Buddy
Something like that
Supposed to be a Duke
Lives out there with his servant
Not a care in the world

DEATH

Met him on that knoll west of town
Where all are imbedded in the ground
Must be an ancient sacrificial place
He was just standing there, contemplating
Maybe enjoying the sun
Said he was waiting for a friend
Didn't say who
Strange guy, mysterious

FLOWERS IN THE MEADOW

We've all seen them
Beginners in life
Bobby K and Eddie M
Never forgotten, so young

Forty did attend
I was the oldest

Soon, I'll get to see
My civil ride with death
Past the fields of grazing grain
Watching the horses heads and breaths
Will I return again?

I too will see circumference and the rose
I too will view the carriage of Death
It passes at my glance
I too will wander barren eternity
Find a path
My voice is there; it leaks through my heart

BEFORE AND AFTER

After the wind—pause
After the rain—the spray
After the lightning—awe
After the thunder—May

After the handshake—greed
After the kiss—anger
After the time—deception
After the crisis—phantoms

Too late—two words
Not comprehended
Like irreconcilable differences
Or non-compatibility

It's over—is spring
Or the gargle of a bird?
Does light die
Celestial Harmony not heard?

THINKING

My soul is a bit disheveled
Thinking many thoughts
Figuring out and planning
Ways of the world for naught
To defeat maladies
And not be defeated
The redundancy of it all

I've looked at thoughts from inside out
Their secret comings and goings
They have such a propensity
And a will for their own doings

I've seen my thoughts from the bleachers
On the drill field, in parade
With drums and bugles in the front
And prisoners from the stockade

DAY OF DIVORCE

Everyone staggers to get the job done
Get the forms finished
Review the proceedings
Day of Divorce has come

The courthouse is like a mausoleum

Amherst
September 25

Illusions in eastern Iowa

WALT WHITMAN

Here is the Heartland Buddha,
Here is the Heartland Spirit,
Here lives the Mid-America Soul.
Here are our carpenters with curious tools;
Our electricians and "The Body Electric";
Bricklayers and mortarboards;
The stone shaper's flying chips;
The tin, tin, tin of the tin roofer;
The grand gravel dumper;
The gravel spreader dressing
Washboard ways of dust and mud.
Here is the Farmland Buddha:
We chop wood, carry trash;
Shuck corn, gather beans.
Here are the raised hogs;
The chickens, the gathering of eggs;
Our cows and cattle are here.
Field mice live indoors in winter;
Here are adopted cats, a lonely dog's howl;
Here feed the red-breasted woodpecker
And the shaggy sparrow.
Raccoons help themselves,
Turkey vultures pirouette;
Here coyotes, snakes, and red foxes live.
Here are our deer aplenty
With ticks and Lyme disease.
Ours is a Mississippi River Deity:
With bluffs, with hills, with patchy forests.
Here are our expansive bridges,
Here are our river lookouts and
Our Grand Dad Bluff.
Fishermen fish for walleye;
Captains and hands steer tugboats and barges;
Paddle wheelers paddle up stream and down stream.

Here are our fish bait cabins, lock and dam #8;
Gamblers gaming on the river.
Ours is a little town Christ:
Night trips from New Albin, Lansing;
Treks to Decorah, Highlandville;
Waukon is our county seat;
The upper Iowa runs through it.
Here we gather together:
Girls at Girl Scout Camp;
Here are our beer parties near the creek,
In the taverns.
Here is where our hermits live
In old log cabins.
Ryumonji is here with
Monks in brown and black robes.
The moon is our delight,
Stars are so abundant.
It's how we live:
We live in the clear blue sky,
On the ocean's floor,
As grains of sand on Ganges' shore,
In each and every leaf of grass,
Each leaf is connected to the sod,
Is connected to the soil,
Is connected to the earth,
Is connected to the sun and planets,
And outward and upward.
Here we spread our arms wide
With open hands,
In every degree and minute;
Here we gather all to our breast, our bosom;
Here we gently hold all.

A MOTHER'S END

A year after the death of her husband,
I could see that her heart had grown
A home for her sorrow: her step was shaking,
Her breathing was work. Still she enjoyed pushing
A supermarket cart and dining out
In Greek and Italian family restaurants.
She watched her weigh, and gained it.
Food was living life: sauerkraut,
Sausage, roasts, sweet potatoes,
Filled cakes, and an open bag of candy
In her coat pocket. And money was loose
And in checks, for me, the grand kids, neighbors,
Nuns, Catholic charities, and Las Vegas.

On the Day of All Souls, the day before
The election of the President;
She came to Loyola in a cab, and a Mother's end begins.
Open her chest, her heart, and by-pass
That sorrow they said; and she at seventy-eight
Asked about the market and the mall? Yes,
They promised; they were in the future
And she with age and trust said do it.
When hope has tears in its eyes,
And gives in with wobbles and fluttering,
Or when the jaws of law or science once
Clutch the sleeve, will ceases and we leave the room.
The operation took place in the middle of the evening.
The next day she was sedated:
Air was pumped into her nose through a tube, bags
With thin lines, like clear vines, trailed under
A heavy blanket and a pump helped the heart,
Soon the kidneys struck. We were
There and sometimes she with her tears was there ,
Anger mixed. Worst than we knew

Said the practitioner, but let's pass on:
A little dialysis, a new balloon (the first
One is leaking), more meds, who knows,
Two, three months, good as new? We visited:
Lamented cried with anguished thoughts and decided;.
We put her in privacy away from the other elders,
From the intense room; and a priest came with oil
And said be stern, ask the surgeon to let her go;
But he said, "We don't do euthanasia here!"
We replied, "Don't do it for us; do it for Mom."
They only kept a monitor which merely
Worried until a final buzz.
Her face turned from life to grey death.

THE TAO

A woman walks up the stairs,
The stairs to the train platform;
Everyday walks up the stairs,
The stairs to the train platform.

Waiting waits for the train;
Everyday waiting waits for the train.
Watching watches down the track,
Watching watches for the train down the track.

A man climbing climes a pole,
Looking looks climbing a pole,
Looks waiting climbing a pole,
Waiting waits climbing a pole.

IT WAS THE YEAR

It was the year __.
It was the year after the year of the suffering year:
The cutting year, the Cancer year, the poison year,
The burning year,
The cutting year.

It was a sunshine day, maple trees in sunshine;
It was patio sunshine.

Maybe it was the suffering year, maybe not;
Maybe it was Osho, maybe not.

He stands in the yard as a fourth tree;
He stands on the patio deck:
The trees stand on the ocean's floor,
Hands swim up and down in the ocean,
Cars swim in the ocean,
People swim in the ocean,
Telephone poles swim in the ocean.

Incense smoke waves in the ocean,
Flags wave in the ocean,
Pictures wave in the ocean,
Flowers wave in the ocean.

It was the year __.

THE DOG

The dog
Runs blindly
Right up to the wheel
Of the semi
Which veers slightly
To the left.
The dog
Catches himself,
Disappointed.
He side-steps toward the porch
Where a woman,
Sweeping,
Scolds him.

The forest

A FRIEND

I heard his buzz below me,
And he stopped on the sleeve of my sweater
Wrapped around my waist.
His white mouth and black and tan face
Looked up at me, and then they seemed
To fold in upon themselves.
The vertical and horizontal stripes on his back
Twitched ever so slightly,
And his outstretched angel wings
Tilted to my left.
We dozed together.
Refreshed, he turned and buzzed away;
And I too turned and climbed the steep hill.

SQUIRREL HEAVEN

In the forest there is danger and wonder.
Rounds are falling from every direction:
Ping and thunk, thud and clink.
The paths are sprinkled with spent shells,
Whose backs resemble beetles,
And crunch like beetles too.
One hardly sees a squirrel about;
They're hidden in their dragon dens;
Upon their golden hoards they lounge,
With protruding bellies,
Like old Buddhas.
There's a joyful bird that sings when it flies,
And a rust-colored leaf that follows
Its own path to the earth,
There's a breeze like the breath of a dying man.

THE FOREST IS GREEN AND GREEN TODAY

The forest is green and green today,
Every single wave is still:
It's Sunday.
The winged people remain snuggled below deck,
A magical mist hangs over all.
Soon slim raindrops will fall
And bring joy to the way.
The singing will begin.
My two churning props are the only sounds;
Then a single, "On the port side" echoes as a runner passes;
Strange meteorites fall into the greenness.
It is a sad sail into the green today,
For its heart is in the houseboat
Of three daughters near an island far upstream.

ELIZABETH

It's raining again today,
The third day.
The mud on my boots from the trail
Is washed down city streets.
Creatures are beginning to form lines,
Two by two.
It has always been so.
Elizabeth, you didn't make coffee this morning;
We missed you.
Your blinds were still down
As we trickled past.
'Tis good to sleep in in the rain,
For awareness arises,
The mind listens,
And watches.

MORNING

Marsh grasses bow their heads to God,
Twitters and coos are heard in the woods,
The creek giggles over its rocky dip,
The eye which sees in winter is blocked.

One Being gives way to all that is.
A pool is kissed by a fish's lips,
A pebble is thrown into a pond.

A dog's harsh bark alarms the sky,
A gunshot pounds the air,
A dog whines while a woodpecker picks,
Dandy lions line the way home.

Redwing blackbirds swing on cattail stalks;
From time to time, red birds wing past.

RETRIEVER

There's a man
In a Wisconsin sweatshirt
Who's tossing a stick
For a Golden Retriever.
Sometimes it retrieves,
Sometimes it watches,
And the man retrieves.

OXYGEN FOR ROBERT

My strident stride
Softened as I came
Out of the woods
And crossed the sunshine
(With the drums of the college
Marching band as background).
As I sat near the fire pit,
A yellow leaf with brown patches
Floated down onto the tip of my shoe
I put the leaf in my notebook:
Oxygen for Robert Young.

A WOODPECKER

A woodpecker pecked on a hollow tree.
No! He pounded on it; he hammered it;
He assaulted it like it had wronged him
In some way. It was his enemy.
The harsh hollow sound engulfed
The silent forest creatures and the nearby trees.
He didn't care; his consciousness
Was entirely captured by this tree,
And his hatred for it.

The marsh

A SINGLE ORANGE-BREASTED ROBIN

A single orange-breasted robin
With an extended stomach
Pecks at the pebbles near the road,
And there is also a song sparrow
With a white feather in its mouth.
I wonder what that is all about?

THIS WAYWARD MONK

This wayward monk
Has lost his robe,
Divorced from the temple gate;
He wanders in the marsh,
Like a crooked creek,
With the birds and the trees.
He recognizes a friend's face
In a newsletter.
How well she looks,
Curly hair, simple smile,
Badge of Buddhism round her neck:
She's on a cold winter retreat
Near a frozen pond.
Who can say the only right Way?

MOMENT

Too subtle for the human eye
It passes swiftly
Suddenly buds are leaves
Skeletal trees are bursting green
Chicks are adults
The sun burns longer as
Young men are old
Beauty—in the blink of the beholder
Is silent
The silhouettes of life
Come to the fore

CARDINAL

Took my binoculars today
Like a real birdwatcher
To see colors, shapes, and plumage.
It was a grey windy back-chilling morn;
Three vociferous geese were flying low.
I sat on a bench
And I waited. I waited…
And then—
From Barnum and Bailey
A most colorful character:
Tufted Punk Rocker hair,
Yellow mouth,
And black beard.
His body was red with a redder breast.
The library's field guide announces him:
Cardinal, Cardinalis.

IT'S GOOD TO BE ALONE IN THE NIGHT

It's good to be alone in the night,
Where silence seeps into my soul,
And two are made one.
How can the cares of the world
Disturb this peace?
Night's quiet breeze cradles the granary
Planked together c1911,
Home now for a solitary sojourner
Through the fields of life,
Torn, bruised, and crumpled.
The morning coffee is good,
As are the poems by Ovid,
Field guides and the cloudy sky:
Night's silence inhabits the day.

The city

SHE WALKED LIKE A MANNEQUIN

She walked like a mannequin
If a mannequin could walk:
Only the joints of her knees appeared to bend.
Her straight blond hair hung down
To the top of her shoulder,
And just the tip of her nose led the way.
Her dress was black
With a thin white belt around her waist,
That divided her in two.
She must have walked right out
Of a store-front window.

THE MEDITATION BELL

The golden bell, like the cup of a chalice,
Rests on its black circular pad
In a corner created by a table and a wall.
The bell waits for the wooden striker to strike it.
When struck, its wondrous call,
Like a Siren's call,
Echoes and re-echoes in the silent room.

THE TREE

There is a twisted and knurled tree
That grows in front of the library.
It's planted in a concrete planter
Waist-high above the way.
Its roots, bulbous, like anomalies,
Are seen above the dirt.
On its trunk there are two main branches,
And the gray round scar of another.
Its many middle limbs
Form a canopy unto themselves,
While those above reach randomly upward.
Its leaves are neither green nor gray,
But somewhere in between.
The tree's lower shelves
Hold tan and shriveled leaves,
Or none.

PEACE

"I marshaled all my thoughts today
And marched them out in sweet array.
The bleachers were of depth and wide
And viewed each nod so none could hide.

"'Twas a gayful crowd and mighty strong
That turned about to dance a song;
But some held forth a need to shine,
And some held on to the hold of "mine."

"The grey clouds drifted to the east,
And snow began its quiet feast.
The earth turned from its brown to white,
And day forgot that night was night.

"Now thought and dance and shinning bright
Were covered by the sky's delight,
And swans of whiteness stood about
In fields of light without a doubt."

CARLY

I walk city streets at a lonely pace;
The "For Rent" sign nods as I pass it.
I look for you at the busy market
At three o'clock, you're not there.
The lights seem out of place and shadowy,
Everyone bustles about.
Something is amiss:
The credit cards refuse to swipe,
Plastic bags fall from their hooks,
And darkness stretches back to the dairy.

A SAD LITTLE TREE

A sad little tree
Shelters my brother.
A government stone,
With a small flag,
Marks his place.
A nearby water spout
Fills flower pots.
A long time gone now,
So young—silver-grey hair,
Face tanned by the sea.

MY OLD FRIENDS

My old friends
Remember the times:
The names of the four girls
In eighth grade,
Penny, who I dated one New Year's Eve,
Loss of sight in one of her eyes,
A stray arrow;
Memories lost to me.

PAST LIVES

Curling black fingers grip the night;
Through their cracks white crests appear.
With the rise and fall of swell against its hull,
A grey behemoth lurks near
A downward slanting dock
Where a ghost, textured in black,
Speckled with spots of spray, like bullet holes,
Watches.
A flash, like a puff of fire, illumes a rusted rail;
Sound, like a tap of air, vibrates:
A shapeless spectre falls....

Near a marble column in burning brightness,
Upholding a sacred arch,
A gold trimmed toga encases a darkly man.
Voices echo in the distance.

CITADEL

High beyond the cityscape,
Boxed in and safe,
Except for the gusty winds
And dust, and the shadows of pigeons
Gliding south.
Viewpoints to the east, to bluff,
To forest, and to spire.
Citadel:
Bringing peace from the rushing dead,
Temporarily, 'till twilight descends
Driving me out to frolic and booze
On pearls where youths and crews wander
Starry-eyed and numb-drugged.
Yet, only for moments,
In vain I looked and then
I withdraw into memories, dreams, and illusions
As the elevator ascends
Into the sky, the sky.
My spirit falls, alone,
To swim in the blueness,
To smell the whiff of death
Trailing in its wake.
Oh stratus, oh nimbus,
Surround my soul with purity,
Return it to its citadel.

Transformations

ANUBIS

Anubis dark more dark then tar,
With snout prolong, ears black and sleek,
Eternal judge of all who sleep,
Egyptian god present tonight.
Bedclothes writhed, hands lash out,
Your head in profile near my bed,
Alive, atremble near death's draft,
Red digit time, the witch's hour.
What omens, signs, portents bring you:
A future futile, desolate?
You speak no word but still I hear
Calypso's call to drink the brew
Of river Styx and pick the daisies
Along its bank in tropical Hades.

RED VIOLETS

For you I pick red violets
Free from around the marsh's fringe
And warm their stems in a walnut bowl
Made by a friend in Salem town

Red petals hug the brim like hearts
Of ladies waiting for their loves
To turn from wars, while wives with babes
In arms wail outside the Iron Gate

They tug at hems of husbands friends'
Thin robes recruits with bows unstrung
And arrows hung in belts they march
Out of the gate toward the Western Realm

They stream onto the wooden bridge
Across the creek and up the hills
Under the moon the columns pass
Away

ECSTACY

In this ninth poem like all the rest
You'll not thrill to an ascending note
That throws you in to ecstasy.
What you'll hear are screeching geese
A mate calls to his loyal wife
Who echoes him like Echo's him
Or two wood ducks in the melodic stream
Or the tone of an Amish horse's hooves.

There's nothing here unusual
Just fine sand in an hourglass
As sun and showers fill the day.

We have our favorite god that's true
But mighty Zeus for yearning minds
Is way beyond our range of thought.

HEAT

We suffer with a Pharaoh's curse
The sun is up its rays rave down
The blueness of the sky is stark
Creek banks are bare, lands raise mid-stream

Spring time has stopped, the buds now wait
Shrunk leaves are stunned, a hermit tree
Now prays for rain, the grass grows not
Cows cry to fields as clouds come by

And pitter-patter for less than a minute.
Will summer bring a heat so hot
It burns the bare path to the pool that's
Filled with wet hot steam, the sky

A space cleared by a tortured God
For a contrary king, a demiurge?

JOHN

South of the deck a maple maligned
With crooked trunk and crooked limbs with
Compound leaves a nothing tree
Landlord wants to cut it down.

Its sap gives soup, it feeds the Jays
In winter deer, songbirds love it they
Fly in space, and there is John
His constant cup of Mountain Dew

to keep his high for dumpster dives
In a college town. Incarcerated for
Pointing a BB gun as coeds run
A coffee house nearby. Released

Seen dusting shelves at Dharma Books
A big gapped-toothy wave to all.

MARS

Because blood Mars is in the twelfth house
Raw anger is hiding in the depths of the psych;
An asp that killed Cleopatra the queen
Is coiled around itself whose fangy venom

Like Lysergic acid burns the mind. The soul
Is carried down to instinctual domains
Venting air, blowing steam, craving
Release from rigor, cuffs, sedateness, PC.

The screams of "Go team go and kill 'em dead"
Resound to gladiators on the field
In throbbing bits in radio waves that bounce
Around and vibrate in prehistoric brutes:

The Neanderthal of dreams to dream new juice
To pillage and plunder like the hero Odysseus.

I AM

To be who I am is to heed
My dark ancestral light built in
To who I am
The womb that points my step this way
Determined by my fate to be
Who I am

Sometimes I happily follow these prompts
Through woods: I read the trees, the sky
But mostly my eyes are shut tight
I'm absent from the one I am
In the stream that runs through me, increased
By who I am

MOTHER'S DAY

We sang a dirge
Then sank into ourselves
The ground was strewn
With fall's bright residue

Silver rails flanked
The grave like prison bars
The rain splattered
On the canopy

Overhead the day's moon
Dawned through the clouds
The lightening and thunder
Had moved to the east

The wind calmed itself
In honor of the occasion
There we stood beside
The open earth

The cold embraced our
Bundled up backs
Each in our own
Thoughts of her and us

A priest intoned a prayer
We said Amen
We did not wait for
The lowering

Sunday came, a peaceful day
On cue the sun appeared
We spoke with silent
Voice of her, our Mom

No one ever completely
Leaves this home
No one will ever love
Us like our Mom

PENELOPE

Wet melancholy morning inexplicable
As a thunderstorm or a clear Narcissus pool
The sun below the rim waits not for Mood
To cast off Dim but hurls into the Day.

The town of contrails, jumping fish, and hearths
To dispel Distraught: the Laws of Nature
Without end, Amen. Circumspect
Athena's child, Penelope, you visit.

You search as subtle as a soft silk gown
For serendipity; you probe deep caves
And dank corners of minds with the primal gift
Of intuition from Artemis, from Hera.

By day you spin by night you cogitate
You plan the weaving cloth to explicate.

A SIMPLE SONG

Today I need to meditate
Upon my old and worn out fate
My mind's been busy as of late
On things both new and out-of-date

A quiet time will do me good
Refreshing now my soul's real food
And point me to a solitude
To heights where I once calmly stood

Now days pass quickly in this old age
They hurry toward the final stage
Where saints and sinners turn the page
To see the way to peace or rage

What else is one called on to do
The skies are dark the days are few
No sense in kneeling in life's pew
'Tis best to stir the pot of stew

A Ghost Story in Three Acts: Imagination verses Reality

I live constantly in the fear of not being misunderstood.

Oscar Wilde

CHARACTERS

(In order of appearance)

Robert (Torch) Torcherelli, aged 42, childhood friend of

Matthew (Matt) Benedict

Sarah Benedict, Matt's daughter, aged 8

Peter (Professor) Apostle, aged 57

Baruch Spinoza, as ghost, aged 40

Hugo Boxel, as ghost, Spinoza's correspondent, aged 40

Cathy, Sarah's friend and neighbor, aged 8

Plato, Sarah's dog

Chatty, Sarah's doll

ACT ONE

Scene One

Family room at Torch's house: couch, coffee table, large TV tuned to a baseball game, sound is off; patio doors; bookcase with trophies, plaques, some books. Torch on couch, Matt on floor leaning against couch. Each glances now and then at the TV.

TORCH: God damned Cubs! Every year it's the same story: Spring training comes, "This is our year, blah, blah, blah;" and then... nothing. Bunch of losers. Know what happened last year?

MATT: No, what happened?

TORCH: Here they are, Cubs and Brewers, neck and neck for the Central Division lead; and then, just like that *(snaps fingers)*, I get a case of the shingles. Can't sleep for two weeks; two weeks! Can you believe it? Ever had shingles?

MATT: I can't say that I have; only heard of them just recently. Another mysterious disease, I suppose.

TORCH: Don't suppose. I had 'em. You don't want 'em. Doc said they're caused by nervous tension.

MATT: Say, did I tell you about my big event from a couple of weeks ago?

TORCH: What big event?

MATT: Well, you remember how hot it was about that time, 100 degrees or so, bright sunshine. I'm sitting in a wicker chair on the patio deck, hoping that a breeze will come along; and I look over toward the maple trees in the backyard, and a man is standing next to the nearest tree. So I look real hard to see who he is. Guess who he is? He's me, myself. I'm standing next to the tree! But I'm sitting on the patio. So I say to me, "This is ridiculous!" I seem to be unable to find the one who is the who who sees!

TORCH: You should hear how you sound. You're turning into an owl.

MATT: *(pause)* Anyway, how can I be there and here at the same time? Then I realize that I'm not on the deck. In fact, I don't know where I'm at; I've lost myself! Two hours later I find me again, but I'm not on the patio; I'm sitting on the floor in the bedroom. I have no idea how I got there. But that's not all. When I raise up my hands in front of me *(raises his hands)*, it's like they're in water, water is running between my fingers. I can't believe it! Not only my hands, but everything is under water, on the bottom of the ocean. When I go to the mall, everyone, whether sitting, standing, or walking, is under water! This goes on for about a week, and then everything returns to normal. You know, I think this is what is called Enlightenment, a Buddha experience. I think this is what those ancient Greeks, wise men like Thales or Anaximander or Parmenides, were talking about. Even Isaac Newton thought that all things were grounded in something that he called the aether.

TORCH: I don't know any ancient Greeks; I've heard of Newton. If you ask me, I'd say all of those guys that you just mentioned were inhaling too much of that aether; they were flying in thin air; and Jeez, Matt, you're right up there with them! You see a mirage and floating images and you call it Enlightenment. And what do you mean by Enlightenment? So now you're a Buddha? You don't look like a Buddha. Hell, look at this *(stands and holds up his stomach with his hands)*, I look more like a Buddha then you *(sits down again)*. I think you're reading too many of those crazy books, and you're going bonkers. Who are you reading now?

MATT: Baruch Spinoza.

TORCH: Baruch Spinoza! Who the hell is Baruch Spinoza?

MATT: A 17th century Rationalist Philosopher, a thinking man's thinking man. He proved that God exists because the universe is Intelligent. You know, all facts have explanation, and God can explain everything.

TORCH: Ya, well, let him explain the Cubs; better yet, how about a miracle and let the Cubs win the pennant! Like I said, you read too much, think too much. Pretty soon you'll be headed for a rubber room! They'll have to put padding on the ceiling; its nuts! What you need is another wife, or at least a girlfriend.

MATT: Perhaps you're right; it was probably the heat and I was seeing mirages. I never did believe in specters. Why would I believe in my own ghost? I've always been more of a rationalist, like Spinoza.

(They continue to talk.)

(Fade out)

ACT ONE

Scene two

Sarah and Matthew in the breakfast area of Matthew and Sarah's condo; table, chairs (4), three windows forming a bay, through them the driveway and front entrance can be seen; large window looking out onto the back yard. The kitchen is seen in the background. A see-through counter and cabinets separate the two areas.

SARAH: *(looking out window into backyard)* Daddy! Daddy! There's a strange man in our backyard!

MATT: Where?

SARAH: He's strange, Daddy; he's just standing there next to the maple trees.

MATT: *(going over to look for him)* I don't see anyone. It's just your imagination. I should never have told you about seeing myself next to the maple tree.

SARAH: *(looks again)* Well, now he's gone.

Front doorbell rings.

Matt goes to see who is there, voices clearly heard (offstage). Sarah stands at the entrance to the kitchen; she is visible.

MR. APOSTLE: I'm sorry to disturb you, but I saw your For Sale sign, so I thought that perhaps you would show me the inside of your house? My name is Peter Apostle.

MATT: Peter *the* Apostle!

MR. APOSTLE: No, no, just Peter Apostle, without the the.

Sarah giggles, then quickly covers her mouth.

MATT: Well, Mr. Apostle, please come in. My name is Matt Benedict and this is my daughter, Sarah. We're just finishing lunch, so you're not interrupting anything. Come into our eating area and sit for a moment.

They enter the area adjacent to the kitchen. Sarah takes her former seat near the rear window. Mr. Apostle sits in an apparent empty place; his back is to the driveway. Matt remains standing.

MATT: Can I offer you a glass of iced tea, Mr. Apostle?
MR. APOSTLE: That would be kind of you. It is a warm day.

Matt goes into the kitchen.

SARAH: *(To Mr. Apostle)* I saw you in our backyard, but when I looked again, you were gone. My Dad saw a ghost right where you were standing next to that tree.
MATT: *(from kitchen)* Sarah! Mr. Apostle is here to look at our house.

Matt, carrying the iced tea, reenters eating area.

MR. APOSTLE: Well, Sarah that sure is a coincidence. I happen to be reading about ghosts right now.
MATT: What book are you reading, Mr. Apostle?
MR. APOSTLE: It's not a book as such; I am reading an exchange of letters between Baruch Spinoza and his friend, Hugo Boxel. Boxel believes in ghosts, but Spinoza doesn't believe in them.
MATT: That really is a coincidence; I'm reading Spinoza's *Ethics*, his treatise on God, the mind, the emotions, and blessedness.
MR. APOSTLE: Then you must know that when Spinoza was expelled from the Jewish Synagogue, he changed his name, which means blessed, to the Latin version, Benedict, You did say that your last name is Benedict, didn't you?

SARAH: Does this mean that we are blessed, Daddy?

Matt gives her a happy smile, but says nothing.

MR. APOSTLE: If you're reading Spinoza's *Ethics*, you will not find any ghosts in there; but he does say some strange things.

MATT: You sound like you are quite familiar with Spinoza and his writings. May I ask you what is your profession?

MR. APOSTLE: I am a professor at the college. My specialty is history, but I am also interested in philosophy; and I have read some theology. Now that you know what I do, you can call me Professor instead of Mr. Apostle. Everyone calls me Professor.

SARAH: What strange things are in the, ah…treaty, Mr. Apostle?

MATT: That's tre-tis, Honey. A treatise is a long discussion about something.

SARAH: OK, tre-tis.

PROFESSOR: As far as strange things in the treatise, Spinoza wrote that everything that makes up a body is eternal; that is matter, the stuff out of which everything is made always has been and always will be. That if one particle of matter is destroyed, then all matter, everything that is made up of matter would end, just like that *(snaps his fingers)*. However, that little "if" will never happen. Spinoza also said the same thing about thoughts, or ideas, or thinking. He said that everything thinks, from the smallest particle to the largest sun, everything has thoughts.

SARAH: Does my dog, Plato, think?

PROFESSOR: Certainly, but not in the same way as your Dad or you think. Your dog knows what he likes, such as dog food and treats; and he knows what he does not like, such as bigger dogs that can hurt him. So your see, your dog tries to stay alive as best as he can, for as long as he can. Spinoza said that this effort to stay alive is life, or the Life Force.

MATT: You mean like 'The Force be with you' from Star Wars?

PROFESSOR: Yes, like that, but in today's world, we have Harry Potter's Magic.

MATT: I don't know much about Harry Potter, Professor.

SARAH: Neither do I..., yet. *(She looks at Matt and smiles with a closed mouth).* So my doll, Chatty, does she think?

PROFESSOR: According to Spinoza, she thinks, but not as a human being can think.

SARAH: Can the planet Venus think?

PROFESSOR: Not as a whole planet. Look at it this way. Each particle of matter, of stuff, has a code within it, and this code tells the particle to get together with other particles that have the same code; and when they all get together, there is Venus. If a particle does not have this special Venus code, then that particle has to move on to find other particles like it; and then they become something else. All of these codes are built into every particle, and they have to follow the rules.

SARAH: Wow that is something weird! OK, do ghosts have particles?

PROFESSOR: Well, there you have me, Sarah. I do not know what a ghost is. Do you know?

SARAH: My dad knows; he saw one in the backyard *(Looks at Matt again),* and I've read about them in books, so they must be, right?

MATT: I think we have to move along here, Sarah. The Professor wants to see our house, ah...condo. Why don't you check on Plato in the back hall, and then go out to the side yard and move the sprinkler to another place where the grass looks dry. In the meantime, I'll show the Professor around our condo.

(Sarah goes out)

MATT: Plato has been not well lately. The vet gave him some medicine and said that he'll be alright in a few days.

(The Professor and Matt return to the hallway).

ACT ONE

Scene three

Baruch Spinoza and Hugo Boxel, as ghosts. An empty stage with a fabricated wall, mid-stage, built to resemble a real wall.

SPINOZA: *(somewhat pompous)* You know I do not believe in ghosts, Boxel. I think apparitions, specters, and ghosts, and the like are fabrications of children and madmen. Narrators use them in order to fit special circumstances where these authors are ignorant of the reality of things or to dispel obvious contradictions in their stories.

BOXEL: I think they do exist. Is not the soul separate from the body, and it is a spirit when the body ceases to be? Besides, they resemble God more than His embodied creatures.

SPINOZA: For me, Boxel, bodies and souls are one. *(They walk though the wall.)*

BOXEL: That's not what you wrote in your treatise. You said thoughts are eternal and they exist in God's Mind.

SPINOZA: True thoughts, my man, not fabrications, imaginings, even memory. True thoughts are given to us by God, and they return to Him. They are Eternal.

BOXEL: But are not thoughts spirits?

SPINOZA: God is not just spirit; God is thought and body, inseparable. Everything that exists is made up of both body and thought. One cannot be without the other. There are no ghosts floating around in the air.

BOXEL: What about the Greek Gods; for example Zeus, and the pantheon of the gods on Mt. Olympus; and angels, archangels, cherubim, and spirits?

SPINOZA: Pure imagination, Boxel, superstition.

(Fade out).

ACT TWO

Scene one

A clear stage, a fence, with a gate, mid-stage, Sarah pulling a water sprinkler attached to a hose.

CATHY: *(over the fence)* Hi Sarah.

SARAH: *(Enthusiastically)* Cathy! What are you doing right now, right now, this very instant?

CATHY: Nothing really.

SARAH: You have to come over. I mean, you just have to! A man rang our doorbell; he said that he saw our For Sale sign, and he wanted to see the inside our condo. He said that he was a Professor, but his name is Peter the Apostle. Can you believe it! He's an Apostle!

CATHY: What do you mean, an apostle?

SARAH: You know, a friend of Jesus, and the Rock and all those other things.

CATHY: You're kidding, of course. You always come up with these crazy stories.

SARAH: *(slightly offended)* I'm not kidding. Come see for yourself. Anyway, I don't think he's a man. I think he's a spirit, a ghost. I mean, Peter the Apostle lived two thousand years ago!

(Cathy enters through the gate; and then she and Sarah exit to go inside.)

We hear them in the back hall talking to Plato and to each other, and we see them in spirit form on a screen, stage front.

CATHY: Poor Plato *(reaches down to pet him)*.

SARAH: The Apostle told Dad and me that Plato can think just like us, and that he has The Force with him. And even Chatty, my doll, and the planet Venus can think.

CATHY: Sarah, will you get real. What's The Force?

SARAH: Something about Star Wars. The Apostle said that it's also about Harry Potter. We should get some books about Harry Potter, and then we'd know about The Force. The only thing I know about Potter now is that he's magical, or he does magical stuff. I bet he can tell us about ghosts!

They continue to console Plato.

(Fade out)

ACT TWO

Scene two

Matt and the Professor have finished touring the rooms of the condo and are again sitting in conversation at the table in the breakfast area. They stop their conversation when Sarah and her friend, Cathy, enter.

SARAH: Cathy, this The Apos, ah…I mean the Professor.

PROFESSOR: *(Ignoring the slip)* It's nice to meet you, Cathy.

CATHY: It's nice to meet you too…Professor. Sarah was telling me about all of the neat things you were saying to her and to her Dad.

PROFESSOR: Well, Cathy, I was just explaining to Matthew, Mr. Benedict, about the neat things I found in his and Sarah's condo. I've always had a special interest in doors and the locks on doors. Did you know that a good door has two locks on it, just like this condo's front door? One lock is usually in the door itself, and the other lock would be called a deadbolt lock. Now here is something that you probably didn't know. You can open some double locked doors without a key, like magic. *(Sarah catches Cathy's eye and smiles at her.)* The first lock opens when you 'Do the right thing'. That is, when you obey the rules. The second lock is a little more difficult to open. In order to open it, you need to have a clear mind. A clear mind is a mind that is not all cluttered with old, worn out ideas that are not so important anymore. We like to hold onto the ideas that we think about. They're like our inventions, although they're not. Once we realize that we don't own them, then they are easier to put aside. Does that make sense to you?

MATT: Sounds like Spinoza talking to us.

PROFESSOR: This does come from Spinoza, but cleansing the mind is an idea that has a long history. Another thing that I noticed in your condo was the beautiful chandelier-like fixture in your entrance hall. A good light, especially at the beginning, gives us a lot of confidence; we can see and know things, and we can plan for the future. Therefore, we have more Life Force, more energy, in order to do things, to live better and longer. You most likely have heard of Albert Einstein, haven't you?

MATT: Yes.

Sarah and Cathy look at each other, but remain silent.

PROFESSOR: Then you must have heard of Einstein's Theory of Relativity. Of course, a theory is just the way things are thought to be until they are shown to be different than what they are thought to be.

Sarah and Cathy lock at each other again, like "duh."

Now Einstein's Theory is expressed in a mathematical way. It is $E=MC^2$. The C stands for light; the M for matter or bodies that we can see, and the E is for energy. The theory says that the more we can see and understand matter, the more energy and Life Force we will have; and just the opposite: the darker it is, the less we see and understand, then we have less Life Force. So the best way to live is to tell and follow the truth because the truth is clear and distinct, and truth can be seen.

SARAH: Is everything that we see true, Professor? I mean like my Plato, and even Venus?

PROFESSOR: Surely, your dog is true and right now his life energy is on the low side because he doesn't know what makes him feel sick. As for Venus, I would say that the particles that make up Venus are true, and the planet Venus is also true.

SARAH: Are ghosts true too, Professor?

(The action freezes for two seconds. Spinoza and Boxel, in conversation, appear stage right; then they disappear.)

PROFESSOR: *(looks at Sarah, pauses, and then smiles)* It is something to think about. I hope that I haven't talked too much. Professors have a way of doing that. Thank you for the tour of your condo. It was a pleasure to meet all of you. You have a very nice daughter and neighbor, Mr. Benedict.

All walk to the door. Mr. Benedict and Mr. Apostle shake hands.

MATT, SARAH and CATHY: Goodbye, Mr. Apostle.
PROFESSOR: Goodbye. You may hear from me again, Mr. Benedict.

Matt exits. Sarah and Cathy remain.

SARAH: Well…?
CATHY: I'm not sure if he is Peter the Apostle or not, but he sure sounds like my dad: *(Mimics her dad)* "Obey the rules, tell the truth."
SARAH: My dad too.

They exit.

ACT THREE

Finale

Dusk, Stage left: Patio, Matthew and Sarah are seated in wicker chairs, Sarah holds her doll. Stage right: backyard with three maple trees. Spinoza and Boxel walk near trees.

SPINOZA: So you see, Boxel, all of these writers, such as Homer, and dramatists, like Sophocles, and Aristophanes, are spinning wondrous and extraordinary tales of gods and wandering spirits in order to test our credulity. Some people will believe anything. Alas, these ingenious authors concoct stories that are clever and inventive, but deceptive. They describe a world which is the result of the vicissitudes of Zeus or of chaotic, random chance, pure luck. However, the universe is ordered, not anarchic. The universe is God; God is the universe.

They continue to talk, but no sound is heard.

SARAH: Didn't Mr. Apostle talk about a lot of strange stuff? Some of it was 'way out there' for me. Like the the-or-ee, or whatever, of Einstein. Chatty tells me that she feels real good about what he said about The Force because she knows that she has The Force in herself. Do you think she has it, Dad?
MATT: Certainly, according to the Professor.
SARAH: I can see her, so she must be also true, right?
MATT: Yes *(occupied)*.

Matt looks toward the trees. Suddenly, his face becomes intense and loses its color. Sarah looks at him, then she looks toward the trees, and then at him again.

SARAH: Daddy *(alarmed)* what is it? What do you see *(continuing alarm)*?

MATT: *(After about ten seconds, he finds himself)* You know, Honey, many wise men have believed that there are many strange things. I mean things that are far beyond what we can see and our ability to understand things.

SARAH: You saw something! Didn't you? You saw ghosts near the maple trees! Oh, I knew it! I knew it! They're real! We just have to go to the bookstore tomorrow to buy a Harry Potter book!

MATT: We can buy two Harry Potter books and send one to Torch. Perhaps Potter's magic can help the Cubs.

They hug.

End.

About the Author

Robert Tosei Osterman has been a practitioner of Zen since 1986. He was ordained a Zen Buddhist monk in 2004. He currently lives a quiet life in a converted granary in rural Wisconsin.